NO AR

Golf Legends

```
THE JERRY B. ANNIS LIBRARY

   TO: Mike Cadarette

Congratulations on your
1st Hole In One
May 10, 1993
11th Hole - A.G.C.

Love,
   Your Wife,
      Jayne

October, 1994
```

920
Ita

by Bob Italia

WHITE SCHOOL
ALPENA, MI

Published by Abdo & Daughters, 6535 Cecilia Circle, Bloomington, Minnesota 55435

Library bound edition distributed by Rockbottom Books, Pentagon Tower, P.O. Box 36036, Minneapolis, Minnesota 55435

Copyright© 1990 by Abdo Consulting Group, Inc., Pentagon Tower, P.O. Box 36036, Minneapolis, Minnesota 55435. International copyrights reserved in all countries. No part of this book may be reproduced in any form without written permission from the publisher. Printed in the United States.

Library of Congress Number: 90-083610   ISBN: 1-56239-011-2

Cover Photo by : Wide World Photos
Inside Photos by: Wide World Photos

Edited by Rosemary Wallner

— Contents —

Introduction 5
Super Mex...7
Arnie 15
Slammin' Sam 23
Bobby 31
The Golden Bear 39

Golf Legends — from left to right Arnold Palmer, Gary Player, and Jack Nicklaus.

Introduction

Of all the major sports, golf is one of the most difficult. Golf requires precise timing for a variety of long and short shots. To become a golf champion, a person must have the desire to practice many hours each day. They must have nerves of steel, and have the determination to be the best. By winning many tournaments over the course of their long and outstanding careers, these five golfers have proven that they have what it takes to be champions.

"Super Mex" Lee Trevino

Super Mex

Lee Trevino was born December 1, 1939, in Dallas, Texas. Trevino never knew who his father was. His parents were not married. As an infant, Trevino lived on a farm with his mother, Juanita, his grandfather, Joe, and his two sisters, Anna and Josephine. Joe was a tenant farmer. He did not own the land that he worked on. Joe took good care of Trevino. "My grandfather was the best father I could have ever had," Trevino once wrote.

When Trevino was seven years old, his grandfather got a job as a grave digger in Dallas.

The Trevinos moved into a four-room shack near a lake. The shack had no plumbing, no electricity, and no windows. The kitchen had a dirt floor and no cabinets. But Trevino was happy. It was his first house.

The Trevino shack was surrounded by pasture. Just beyond the pasture was a big green field. Every day, Trevino saw people on the field swinging sticks at a little white ball. Trevino did not know that the green field was the Dallas Athletic Club. He did not know the people were playing golf.

Eventually, Trevino started going to the clubhouse near the golf course. He hung around the caddie shack and learned all about the game of golf. The caddie master hired Trevino when he was eight years old. Now Trevino was making money and helping his family.

As a caddie, Trevino carried golf bags for the members. He earned sixty-five cents for nine holes and one dollar and twenty-five cents for eighteen holes. Sometimes, he got a generous tip. Trevino also played golf and cards with the other caddies.

Trevino caddied for one older man every Sunday. When Trevino and the man were out of sight of the clubhouse, the man would let Trevino play. Trevino always bet his caddie fee—double or nothing—that he could beat the man. Trevino won every time.

In 1956, Trevino, now seventeen years old, joined the U.S. Marine Corps. He played for the marine's golf team, but he still was not thinking about a professional career. After his discharge in 1960, Trevino got a job at Greenwood's Driving Range in Dallas. One day his boss said, "Are you going to be a laborer the rest of your life or do you want to play golf? You have the ability to be a professional golfer and a good one."

The encouragement helped Trevino decide to turn pro. He joined the North Texas chapter of the Professional Golf Association (PGA). He played in many tournaments, most of which he won.

In the summer of 1963, twenty-four-year-old Trevino saw his first PGA Championship tournament. There, Trevino saw Jack Nicklaus play for the first time. Trevino was in awe of

Nicklaus. He had never seen a better player. Trevino decided he wanted to be a great player, too.

In 1965, Trevino found a sponsor to pay his traveling expenses for the Professional Tour. He played in the Texas State Open in Houston, Texas, and won $1,000—the most money he had ever seen. Then it was on to the Mexican Open where he finished second and won $2,100. There, he met his future wife, Claudia. Trevino continued to play small tournaments, winning moderate prize money.

Trevino's first attempt at a major tournament came in 1966 at the U.S. Open. He tied for 54th place and won $600. Discouraged, he avoided the tough competition at the major tournaments. He played smaller tournaments where he could win more prize money. In 1967, when the United States Golf Association (USGA) sent Trevino an entry blank for the U.S. Open, he threw it away. His wife plucked the entry blank from the trash, signed her husband up, and convinced him to play. Trevino played well, finishing fifth. He won $6,000. Now he was ready to join the regular tour.

Lee Trevino throws his cap after he won the U.S. Open Golf Championship title by defeating Jack Nicklaus in an eighteen-hole extra round play.

While tour kings Arnold Palmer and Jack Nicklaus traveled the country in their private jets, Trevino drove to each tournament with his wife in a 1965 Plymouth station wagon. They stayed at inexpensive motels and ate at inexpensive restaurants. But soon Trevino began to make money on the tour, and he kept on driving. By the end of the year, he had won $26,475 and was named Rookie of the Year for 1967.

In 1968, Trevino again entered the U.S. Open. His tee shots were never better and his putting was strong. On the last day of the tournament, Trevino was in second place. He was only a few shots behind the leader, Bert Yancey. Yancey's game fell apart and suddenly Trevino found himself five shots ahead. After some nervous moments, Trevino won the Open, beating Jack Nicklaus by four shots. "Congratulations," Arnold Palmer said to Trevino afterwards, "you've won the big one." Trevino received $30,000. His life would never be the same. Now dubbed "Super Mex," Trevino was one of golf's top players. He would stay at the top for a long, long time.

The next year, 1969, was an off year for Trevino. He only won one tournament, the

Tucson Open. But he still managed to earn $112,418. In 1970, Trevino won two tournaments, the Tucson Open and the National Airlines Tournament. Trevino earned $157,037 that year. He was now the top prize winning golfer. In 1971, Trevino won his second U.S. Open, beating Jack Nicklaus by three shots in a play-off. The following week, Trevino won the Canadian Open. Then it was on to the British Open. Trevino won that, too. The U.S. Open, the Canadian Open, and the British Open—Trevino had won all three.

A year later, Trevino returned to the British Open and won again. In 1974, Trevino added the PGA Tournament to his list of major tournament wins. And then, after years of struggling with a bad back, a drinking problem, and bad business deals, Trevino got his life in order and won the 1984 PGA Championship.

Trevino has won more than thirty-five tournaments. He is fourth on the all-time money making list. Today, Lee Trevino is still on the tour. Having recently turned fifty years old, Trevino became eligible to join the Senior PGA Tour. He will continue to play and hold his title as one of golf's greatest players.

Arnold Palmer sends an iron shot straight down the middle.

Arnie

Arnold Palmer was born September 10, 1929, in Latrobe, Pennsylvania. He lived in a modest home on the Latrobe Country Club where his father, Milford, was greens keeper and club professional.

When Palmer was seven years old, his father began encouraging him to play golf. Milford sawed off part of a golf club and gave it to his son to practice with.

When he was eleven years old, Palmer was giving golf lessons to the club's members. He also was winning the club's caddie tournament on a regular basis.

When he entered Latrobe High School, Palmer immediately made the varsity golf team. In 1943, he played his first match and won. During all four years on the team, Palmer was the number one golfer.

While he was a sophomore, Palmer took third place in the Pennsylvania Junior Amateur. Then he won the district junior amateur and the Western Pennyslvania Amateur. In 1947, Palmer traveled to Los Angeles to play in the National Junior Amateur, but lost. While in Los Angeles, Palmer was persuaded to apply for a scholarship at Wake Forest College in North Carolina, which he received.

Palmer played for Wake Forest's golf team. But when a teammate died in a car crash in 1950, a saddened Palmer quit college and joined the coast guard. Palmer did not play golf for three years.

When he was stationed in Cleveland, Ohio, Palmer made some friends who got him out on the golf course. Suddenly, his passion for golf returned. Palmer even played in the ice and snow of winter. He began to think of playing golf as an amateur.

When his coast guard enlistment was over in 1954, Palmer entered the U.S. Amateur championship in Detroit, Michigan, and won. Three weeks later, he met Winnie Walzer. A week later, he proposed to her and she accepted. Now Palmer had to think of a way to support himself and his wife-to-be. Thoughts of remaining an amateur left him. He knew he had to turn professional. On November 19, 1954, he did just that.

Palmer's first professional win came in 1955 at the Canadian Open. He won by four shots and earned $2,400. In 1956, Palmer won the Eastern Open and the Insurance City Open. Then in 1957, he won the Houston Open, the Azalea Open, the Rubber City Open, and the San Diego Open. Palmer was making good money, but he knew he could win more prize money by winning a major tournament.

In 1958, Palmer entered the Masters tournament and won. By the end of the year, twenty-nine-year-old Palmer had earned an amazing $42,608.

Two years later, Palmer had the greatest year of his professional career. In early 1960, he entered the Palm Springs Desert Classic. On the final day, Palmer made a charge—something he would soon be famous for—from way back in the field. He captured the title and its $12,000 first prize. People cheered wildly. Never had they seen a golfer make such a run for first place.

Palmer won three more tournaments before he arrived at Augusta, Georgia, to play in the Masters. Already, he had won $26,000, and it was only April. On the final day of the Masters, Palmer was tied for the lead after nine holes. The crowds followed him, wondering if he would make a charge for first place. On the eleventh hole, someone held up a sign that read: *Go Arnie...Arnie's Army.* The crowd was with him, cheering him on. Palmer was fast becoming a tour favorite.

Palmer, a tour favorite, talks to his golf ball saying, "Go-go-get in the hole."

On the seventeenth hole, Palmer made his move. He sunk a thirty-five-foot putt for a birdie (one stroke less than par). The crowd—his army—roared their approval. On the final hole, Palmer put his second shot six feet from the flag. As he lined up his putt, his army grew silent. Then he rolled the putt in. The crowd went wild. Palmer had won the Masters again. He had also won the hearts of golf fans everywhere, thanks to the television coverage of the tournament. Suddenly, Palmer was one of the most recognized sports figure in America.

In May 1960, Palmer entered the U.S. Open. After three rounds, he was seven shots behind. But Palmer did not seem to worry. His fans knew he would make a charge.

On the final day, Palmer's charge started immediately. He birdied six of the first nine holes and eventually finished with a 65. The U.S. Open Title was his. He was the first man ever to come from seven strokes back on the final day.

Palmer won two more tournaments that year, bringing his total wins to eight, including two major championships. His total earnings for 1960 was an amazing $75,263.

Palmer won the British Open in 1961 and 1962. More Masters victories came in 1962 and 1964. In 1963, he became the first player ever to win $100,000 in one year. And in 1968, Palmer became golf's first millionaire.

By the end of the 1960s, Jack Nicklaus had replaced Palmer as the king of the tour. And though Palmer's last PGA victory occurred in 1973, he still plays the tour today, especially the Senior Tour.

During his pro career, Palmer compiled sixty-one U.S. titles. His fans—his army—still come out and cheer him, hoping to see one last charge for a tournament win.

"Slammin" Sam Snead

Slammin' Sam

Sam Snead was born May 27, 1912, in Ashwood, Virginia. His father, Harry, was the caretaker for the Homestead Hotel. A big, powerful man, Harry also did some farming. But the Sneads were always poor.

When Snead was old enough, he helped his father on the farm. He shocked wheat and stacked hay. Working on the farm was hard, but Snead was happy. He always had clothes on his back and food in his stomach. All the while, Snead grew strong and tall.

When he was not helping his father on the farm, Snead spent his time hunting. He hiked into the nearby Back Creek Mountains with his gun and iron traps. He hunted fox, rabbit, wildcats, and weasels. Afterwards, he would sell their pelts.

When Snead was seven years old, he shagged gold balls in a cow pasture for his brother, Homer. Homer would not allow Snead to use his clubs, so Snead made his own. He took an old buggywhip, cut the whip from the shaft, and attached an old clubhead to the shaft. It was not much of a golf club, but Snead claimed he could "sock a ball from here to yonder with it."

But the whip was not good enough for Snead. He wanted clubs like his bother had. He cut a branch from a tree and trimmed it. He removed the knots but kept twelve inches of bark for a grip. After attaching an old clubhead to it, Snead challenged his brother to a match. "I got my butt beat," he later wrote.

Snead's formal introduction to golf came one day when a neighbor invited Snead to caddie with him at the nearby Cascades Hotel. "While I was waiting [to caddie]," he later wrote, "I fooled around hitting balls in the yard there.

A lady came in and put a whole lot of dimes and nickels and pennies in my hat and, man, I thought I was the richest person in the world." Golf and money had been linked. Snead was already hooked.

Snead sharpened his competitive skills in high school. He played basketball, football, and participated in track. And, of course, he played golf. The best he ever finished in a high school tournament was third. And twice, he came in second in a longest drive contest, hitting the ball 318 yards.

Snead improved his golf game by playing in the cow pasture. He used carved sticks for clubs and stones for golf balls. He measured his driving using the fence posts that lined the pasture. He would aim at the fence posts and try to hit them. Snead buried tomato cans in the pasture and used them to putt into. Eventually, he set up his own golf course. The chicken pen and the outhouse were some of his course's hazards.

In 1930, Snead got a permanent caddying job at the Cascades Hotel. In 1934, he bought his first set of golf clubs, one club at a time. Now he could practice the game seriously.

By now, Snead was twenty-two years old. His mother thought he should be a tailor. Others thought he should find a skilled labor job. "But I wanted to golf like nothing else," he wrote.

A young man living in the mountains of Virginia did not have much of a chance at becoming a professional golfer. Snead needed money to become a pro, but he did not have any. Snead needed a sponsor.

In 1936, Snead entered the Cascades Open. His 300-yard drives brought astonished whistles from the spectators. He came in third, winning $359. Afterwards, the manager of the Greenbrier Hotel in White Sulphur Springs, West Virginia, offered Snead a job as club professional. Snead gladly accepted.

On his first day at Greenbrier, Snead, playing on the fifth hole, whacked a drive 335 yards. His golf ball struck a man on the green. The man, Alva Bradley, was the owner of the Greenbrier Hotel. When he found out Snead had hit him with his drive, he hired Snead as his personal instructor. Bradley was impressed with Snead's talent. He pledged to sponsor Snead on the professional tour.

*Sam Snead as club professional
plays out of the rough.*

Snead went on to win the West Virginia Open and the West Virginia PGA Tournament. Then in 1937, Snead traveled to Oakland, California, and entered the Oakland Open. On the last day, on the final hole, Snead made a putt for birdie that won him the title and a check for $1,200. A few days later, Snead found his picture in a New York paper. "How'd they get my picture?" he wondered. "I ain't never been there!"

Despite his country boy image, Snead went on to become one of the greatest professional golfers in history. He compiled a staggering 135 tournament wins, including titles at the PGA Championship (1942, 1949, 1951), the British Open (1946), and the Masters (1949, 1952, 1954). In 1965, fifty-two-year-old Snead won the Greensboro Open. He became the oldest player to win a PGA tour event. In 1974, when he was sixty-two years old, he finished third in the PGA Championship behind Lee Trevino and Jack Nicklaus. In 1980, Snead won the Legends of Golf tournament when he was sixty-eight years old.

Snead chips from the edge of the lake into the cup at the twelfth Hole.

Sam Snead has been the PGA Senior champion six times, and the World Senior champion five times. Today, Snead is still on the golf course, no doubt ready to add to his record total of tournament wins.

Bobby Jones

Bobby

Robert (Bobby) Jones, Jr., was born March 17, 1902, in Atlanta, Georgia. His father, Robert, was a successful lawyer. Jones's family was rich. Young Jones had lots of leisure time—especially for golf.

In the early 1900s, golf was a sport of the rich. The Jones family had a cottage near the East Lake Country Club in Atlanta where they spent their summers. Jones was encouraged at an early age to play golf. From the moment he first picked up a club at age five, everyone could tell he was a natural. He seemed to know how to swing properly without having taken a single lesson.

After a few years of following his parents around the golf course, Jones started going out on his own. He eventually was coached by East Lake's pro, Stewart Maiden. But even Maiden could not find anything wrong with Jones's swing. "I taught Bobby as little as possible," he recalled.

When he was nine years old, Jones became East Lake's junior champion. At eleven years old, Jones shot under 80 for the first time. At thirteen years old, Jones won the club championship, defeating his father in the final match. By the time he was fourteen years old, Jones was driving the ball 250 yards with his graceful, fluid swing. Jones decided it was time to see what he could do outside East Lake.

When Jones began to play in tournaments, the matches were played for fun, not for money. That year, Jones entered the Georgia State Amateur Championship and won. Feeling confident, Jones entered the most prestigious amateur tournament of all—the U.S. Amateur, where golfers of all ages played. He won his first two matches before being eliminated.

A year later, Jones won the Southern Amateur. Already some people were calling fifteen-year-old

Jones America's best golfer. In 1919, he came in second in the Canadian Open and the U.S. Amateur. One year later, he tied for eighth at the U.S. Open.

Jones had become a crowd favorite. He was handsome, polite, and well-dressed. And he was intelligent. When he was not playing golf, he studied engineering, mathematics, chemistry, geology, and physics at Georgia Tech University where he received high grades. He continued his studies at Harvard University in Massachusetts. There, Jones studied French and German, history, and English literature. Jones also spent two years studying law at Emory University in Atlanta.

Jones's march into golf's history began in 1923 when he won the U.S. Open. In 1924, he won the U.S. Amateur, then repeated the feat in 1925. In 1926, Jones won the U.S. Open and the British Open. He was the first golfer to win both opens in the same year. Jones returned to the British Open a year later and won again, then captured another U.S. Amateur title. Jones won the U.S. Amateur again in 1928, and in 1929 he won the U.S. Open.

Bobby Jones in 1930; that year he became the only golfer in history to complete the "Grand Slam" of golf.

In 1930, Jones amazed everyone. He won all four major championships: the U.S. Open, the British Open, the U.S. Amateur, and the British Amateur. Winning all four major tournaments in one year is called the "Grand Slam" of Golf. No one but Jones—not even Jack Nicklaus—has ever accomplished this feat.

Strangely, after his greatest year, twenty-eight-year-old Bobby Jones retired from golf. He had never accepted a penny for his amazing efforts. Golf was never very important to him. It was just a sport. Family came first, then his law practice. Jones helped to design the Augusta National Golf Course (the site of the Masters tournament) in Atlanta. He occasionally made appearances in tournaments over the course of the next two decades. But as a regular competitor, Jones had retired.

Bobby Jones died on December 18, 1971, of an aneurysm after being paralyzed by syringomylia, a disease that attacks the spinal cord. His name lives on in the record books as one of the greatest players ever. Jones had won thirteen of the twenty-one major championships he had played in—and he had done it in a span of only eight years. It would take Jack Nicklaus over ten years to catch and pass Bobby Jones's record.

Jones's natural ability and fluid swing made him, by some peoples standards, "America's best golfer."

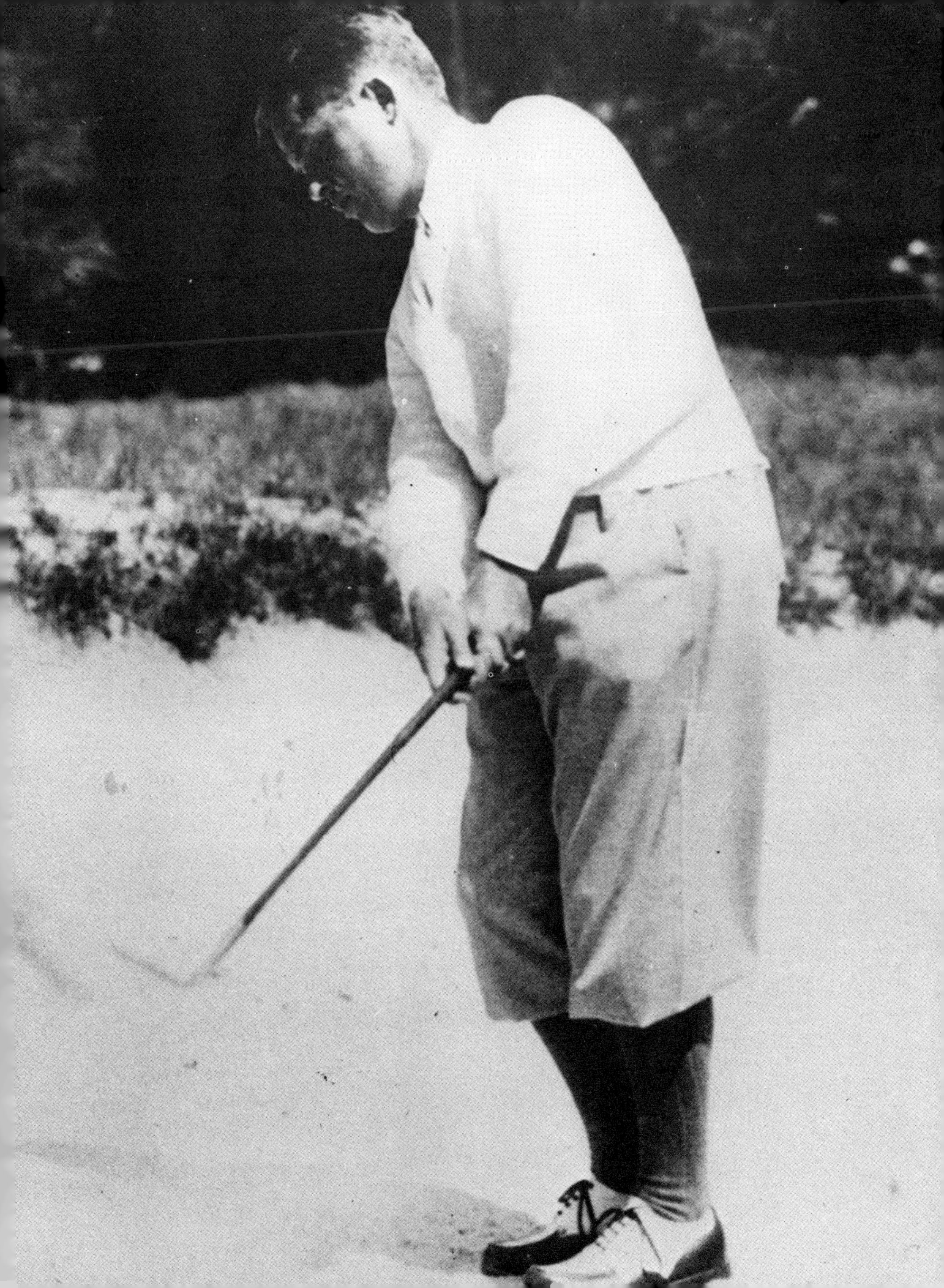

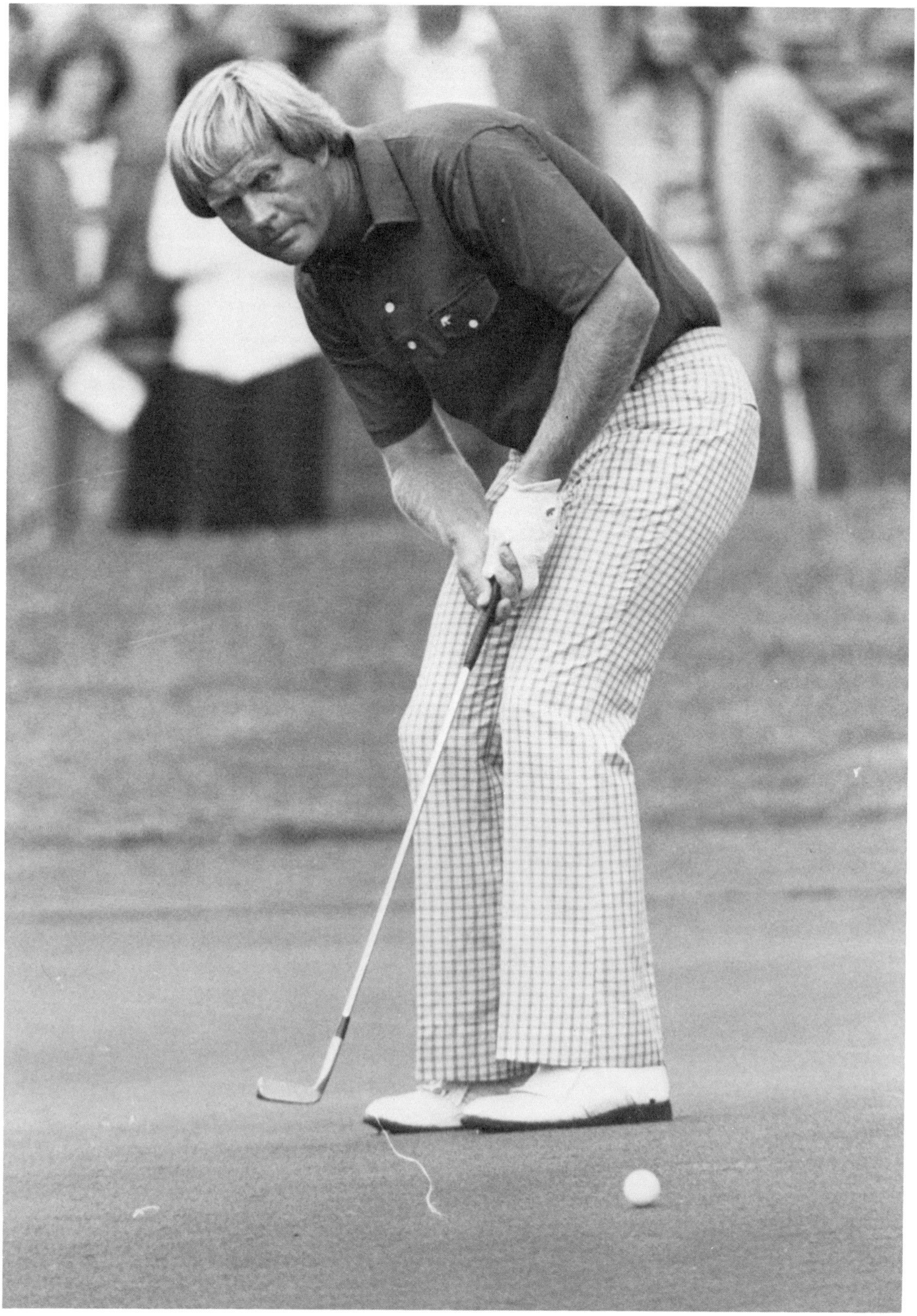

The Golden Bear

Jack Nicklaus was born January 21, 1940, in Columbus, Ohio. Nicklaus lived in a comfortable home. As a young boy, Nicklaus preferred to play outdoors rather than inside. This led him to an interest in golf at an early age. His father, Charlie, belonged to a country club. He encouraged his son's interest in golf. He set up a driving range in the basement of the house and hired a private golf instructor.

Nicklaus played his first nine holes of golf when he was ten years old. He shot a 51, which is very good for a first score.

Jack Nicklaus — The "Golden Bear"

The next year, Nicklaus got his first full set of clubs and eventually shot an 81. Then Nicklaus set his goal to shoot in the 70s, then the 60s. Late one summer afternoon in 1953, Nicklaus played golf with his father. Nicklaus shot 69.

That same summer, Nicklaus grew ill. But that did not stop him from playing in a celebrity tournament. After a few holes, Nicklaus's father came out on the course to take him to the doctor. The doctor told Nicklaus he had polio. The case was not serious and soon Nicklaus was feeling better.

Nicklaus was not just a talented golfer. He also played basketball for his school, Upper Arlington High School. But by the time Nicklaus was sixteen years old, golf was already his life. He practiced long hours—even at night. In 1955, his dedication and hard work paid off. That year, Nicklaus won the Ohio State Open with scores of 76-70-64-72. The second place finisher was a middle-aged professional who finished three shots behind Nicklaus.

Nicklaus's first national title came in 1957 when he won the U.S. Jaycees Junior Championship.

He received a $1,000 scholarship to the college of his choice—Ohio State.

Nicklaus studied pre-pharmacy at Ohio State. His grades were not bad, but he spent most of his time pursuing his sports passion. He played intramural basketball, football, softball, volleyball, and tennis. He joined a fraternity, and met his future wife, Barbara. And of course, he played golf.

As an eighteen-year-old freshman, Nicklaus won the Trans-Mississippi Tournament. He entered his first pro tournament, the Rubber City Open, and finished in 12th place. Then, amazingly, he qualified for the prestigious U.S. Open. He finished in 41st place.

In 1959, Nicklaus won the Trans-Mississippi Tournament for the second time and obtained his most important title by winning the U.S. Amateur. Now Nicklaus was seriously considering a professional golf career. And he was only nineteen years old. With all his success, Nicklaus did not have time to play for Ohio State until the following year.

Jack Nicklaus driving the ball.

In 1960, Nicklaus won more honors and trophies. He finished in 13th place in the Masters. Now Nicklaus was convinced he could become a pro, and he practiced harder than ever before.

In 1961, Nicklaus became the Western Amateur champion. He won the U.S. Amateur for the second time. But all his energies were focused on golf. Nicklaus was away from Ohio State much too often, and this got him into trouble. After his junior year, Nicklaus dropped his pre-pharmacy studies and entered Ohio State's College of Commerce, majoring in insurance.

After he married Barbara, Nicklaus sold insurance to support himself and his wife. Still, Nicklaus was spending too much time pursuing a golf career. Finally, the dean of the college asked Nicklaus to drop out. To this day, Nicklaus regrets not getting his degree. "It's the one big thing in my life that I started and didn't complete," he once wrote.

On November 8, 1961, Nicklaus turned professional. His first official pro tournament was the Los Angeles Open. He tied for 50th place, and received only $33.33. But Nicklaus was not worried. The years of experience and success in amateur golf prepared him for the tour.

Nicklaus was a formidable figure as well. He stood 6 feet, and weighed over 200 pounds. His upper body was powerful and his legs were strong. Since Nicklaus has blond hair, his fans called him "The Golden Bear." Nicklaus could hit the ball farther—and with more accuracy— than anyone on the tour. It would only be a matter of time until he dominated the PGA tour.

Later in 1962, Nicklaus entered the U.S. Open. Hundreds lined the first fairway to see if Nicklaus could beat Arnold Palmer, the current king of the tour. Nicklaus hit his first tee shot long and down the middle. People gasped in amazement. They knew their beloved Arnie was in trouble.

When Nicklaus first turned pro, people did not know what to make of him. They knew Nicklaus had great talent, but he did not seem very polite or nice. The fans booed Nicklaus when he made good shots and cheered when he faltered. This made Nicklaus even more determined to win. When Nicklaus won his first major tournament, his rivalry with Palmer—and the fans—was set.

Nicklaus chipping onto the green.

In 1963, Nicklaus won the Masters for the first time. He had beaten Sam Snead, and again Nicklaus found some fans booing him. Later that year, Nicklaus won the PGA Tournament. In two years, he had won three major tournaments. Not only was he good, he was great. And Nicklaus was only beginning.

Nicklaus eventually overcame his poor image. He made an effort to smile and wave to the crowd. He treated the other golfers with more respect. The fans began to warm up to Nicklaus. They cheered him as he continued to dominate the PGA tour.

During the rest of the 1960s, Nicklaus won the Masters two more times (1965, 1966), the U.S. Open one more time (1967), and the British Open once (1966). When he was not winning, Nicklaus usually finished second or third. By the time the decade was over, Nicklaus had replaced Arnold Palmer as the king of golf.

The 1970s brought even more greatness. Nicklaus was never better. He won the Masters in 1972 and 1975. He won the U.S. Open in 1972. He won the British Open in 1970 and

1978. And he won the PGA Tournament in 1971, 1973, and 1975.

In 1973, Nicklaus broke a record. After he had won the PGA Championship, his total number of major titles (including his two Amateur Championships) came to fourteen—one better than the record holder, Bobby Jones.

The 1980s saw Nicklaus in a state of transition. Many thought he was getting too old to compete on the tour. But Nicklaus won the U.S. Open and the PGA Championship in 1980. And in 1986, he won the Masters.

In all, Nicklaus has won twenty major titles: the U.S. Amateur twice, the Masters six times, the U.S. Open four times, the British Open three times, and the PGA Championship five times. No one, not even Bobby Jones, comes close to Nicklaus's accomplishments. Even more, Nicklaus has won a total of eighty-nine tournaments worldwide. Only recently, because of higher tournament prizes, has Nicklaus been knocked from the top of the all-time money list.

Nicklaus is still playing golf. More titles will undoubtedly be won. For now, Nicklaus limits his playing time to the major tournaments. But with the start of the PGA Senior Tour, Jack Nicklaus will be playing—and winning—for many more years to come.

1987: four-time U.S. Open winner Jack Nicklaus blasts out of the bunker.